Ravenscourt
B·O·O·K·S

Pioneers
of Independence

By

C. L. Collins

SRA

Columbus, OH

Photos: 10, AKG-Images; 22, © Louise Gubb/Corbis SABA; 32, © Reuters/Corbis; 45, AP/Wide World Photos.

Cover illustration: Denny Bond

SRAonline.com

Send all inquiries to this address:
SRA/McGraw-Hill
4400 Easton Commons
Columbus, OH 43219

Printed in the United States of America.

ISBN: 978-0-07-611305-7
MHID: 0-07-611305-1

  3 4 5 6 7 8 9 MAL 13 12 11 10 09 08

The *McGraw·Hill* Companies

Contents

Chapter 1

Independence

*Every year, people in the United States celebrate their country's independence on the fourth of July. They have barbecues and picnics on that day. And they recognize the names of those who helped win the independence of a small group of colonies. Thomas Jefferson, George Washington, and Alexander Hamilton were all part of the United States' struggle for independence. You might hear about them in history class. Their faces are on U.S. money.

But we often don't think about how what they said, did, and wrote created the government the United States has today. People often forget the great bravery it took to stand up to a larger and more powerful force. For the colonies, that power was the British government.

People sometimes forget that keeping independence is a process that never stops. And the United States is not the only place where the work of a few has changed* history. In the past 100 years there have been leaders who worked very hard on the often slow process of changing the way governments work. Sometimes it's difficult to see any progress. We often don't know about the sacrifices they make. Some choose war to gain independence. Others choose a nonviolent path.

Who are these great pioneers of independence?

—Chapter 2—

Mohandas Gandhi

Do you know about Mohandas Gandhi? He led India to independence. Many who came after Gandhi modeled their actions after him. In the United States, Martin Luther King Jr. studied Gandhi's example. But who was this deeply religious Hindu revolutionary? Who was the man who is thought of as the father of his country?

Gandhi was born in 1869 in Porbandar, India. It was a small, quiet place. Porbandar was the capital of a small state. Gandhi's father was the manager of this state. His mother spent a lot of time helping others.

At that time, most of what is now India and Pakistan was run by the British Empire. The British Empire stretched across Africa, Asia, and the Caribbean. India was the biggest colony in the empire.

*Gandhi's father worked in a state that was run by the British. Gandhi's family was Hindu. They believed they should not harm any living thing. Because of this belief, they were vegetarians. They also believed in tolerance toward other religions and beliefs.

Gandhi followed his family's wishes in most things. He did what was expected of him. His family decided he should be a government manager. But Gandhi really wanted to be a doctor. He was not interested in politics. He did not even read a newspaper.

To work for the government, he had to be a lawyer. So in 1888 Gandhi went to England to study law. He was 19 years old. Before he left, he promised his mother he would follow Hindu rules and not eat meat, drink alcohol, or date.

Life in England was not easy. Everything was different. Gandhi struggled with the language. Clothes, food, and* the way of life there were very different. He tried to get used to it. But he could not find vegetarian food because there were not many vegetarians in those days. This was a real problem for him.

Finally he found the London Vegetarian Society. He quickly became a member. There were many interesting people in the society. They had ideas and beliefs that were not like everyone else's. They believed everyone should be treated fairly. Many of them thought they did not fit into English society. Through people in this group, Gandhi was introduced to new ideas. Many of these ideas changed Gandhi's political and moral beliefs.

He read the Christian Bible and the *Bhagavad-Gita*, the Hindu religious guide. In the Gita, two ideas leaped out at him. One was turning away from the search for money and things. Another was working without fear of failing. The Gita said people should try to achieve without worrying about success or failure.

Gandhi returned to India in 1891. He was a lawyer, but he could not find a place for himself. He was too shy to argue before the court. He felt overpowering stage fright when speaking in public. Then he took a one-year contract job at an Indian law firm in Natal, South Africa, in 1893. He was 23 years old.

South Africa was also a colony of the British Empire. South Africa was made up of white colonists, black Africans, people of mixed race, and Indians. People who were not white were thought of as a lower class. There were rules for "whites" and different rules for everyone else.

In South Africa, Gandhi's life would change. Soon after arriving, he went to court to argue a case. The judge asked him to take off his turban. He would not. He walked out of the courtroom.

A few days later he took a train from Durban to Pretoria. On the train, he was told to get out of the first-class coach because it was for white people only. But he did not move. So the conductor threw him off the train. He had to spend the night on a freezing train platform.

Later a stagecoach driver beat him because he would not give up his seat to a white person. Gandhi found that being Indian in South Africa meant being humiliated every day.

After one year, his contract was up. He prepared to leave the country. At a going-away party, he saw a newspaper article about a new law that was being planned. The law would take away the right of Indians to vote in Natal. Gandhi told the other guests that the law could be a nail in their coffins. So they begged him to stay in South Africa and help defend the rights of Indians. And he did.

Gandhi had been afraid of speaking in public. But at the age of 25, he became a tireless politician. He wrote letters and made speeches. He called attention to the lives of Indians in South Africa. He had planned on staying in South Africa for only one year. He ended up staying until 1914.

Gandhi continued to read the books of several religions. In South Africa he worked out many of the ideas and methods he would later use in India. These included passive resistance, nonviolent protest, and peaceful demonstration. One of the main ideas he studied was nonviolently breaking an unjust law to get the attention of those in charge.

A politician in South Africa who battled Gandhi wrote about him in 1918: "Persons in power should be very careful how they deal with a man who cares nothing for sensual pleasure, nothing for riches, nothing for comfort or praise, or promotion, but is simply determined to do what he believes to be right. He is a dangerous and uncomfortable enemy . . . ."

Mohandas (Mahatma) Gandhi with the British
Secretary of State for India and Burma in 1946

When Gandhi returned to India, he was 45 years old. For the next 30 years he worked for India's freedom. He fought for equality and tolerance for all Indians. Gandhi was powerful. He brought many Indian groups into one movement. He quickly became the strongest force in India. He came to be called *Mahatma*, which means "great soul."

Gandhi's course of action was nonviolent noncooperation. He told people not to buy things made in England. He did not cooperate with British courts and parliaments in India. He led efforts to nonviolently break laws that would force arrest.

He was first arrested in 1922. By then, 30,000 Indians had been arrested for nonviolently breaking the law. He was not released for almost two years.

In 1930 Gandhi led one of the most successful efforts against British rule. The British government had passed a law that said Indians could not make their own salt. This was very hard on poor Indians. Gandhi asked Indians to continue making their own salt. After a year, more than 60,000 people had been arrested. Gandhi was then asked to work with the government to try and end the conflict.

In 1942 Gandhi was arrested again. He was not freed until 1945, when he was 74. During his lifetime he spent over six years in prison.

After World War II the British were ready to leave India. For the next two years Gandhi worked to end the violence between Hindus and Muslims that came as British rule was ending.

India finally gained independence in 1947. But to Gandhi, it came at a high price. India was divided into two countries: India and Pakistan. India became a mostly Hindu country. Pakistan became a mostly Muslim country. Gandhi was greatly saddened by the splitting of the country along religious lines.

In 1948 Gandhi was shot and killed. He had preached nonviolence and tolerance throughout his life. He was 77 years old when he died.

Chapter 3

Nelson Mandela

Gandhi's struggle for Indian independence inspired many people. One of the most famous of those he inspired lived in South Africa.

Rolihlahla Mandela was born in 1918 in Qunu, South Africa. Only a few hundred people lived in his village. The village was deep in the *veld*, a wide, flat grassland with few trees. Mandela's father was the leader of Qunu.

Mandela spent his early years playing with other children in the valley. They wore red blankets. Everything they ate they had raised themselves.

Many of the men of the village lived far away. They worked in gold mines and on farms. They worked hard for very little money. They returned only a few times a year to plow the fields in the village. The rest of the time, the women of the village worked in the fields and took care of the children.

One day Mandela and his friends were trying to ride a donkey. When it was his turn, Mandela jumped on it. It ran into a thorn bush and pushed him off. Mandela's face was scratched. Thorns cut his skin. He was embarrassed in front of his friends. After that, he tried to win games without embarrassing the other boys. And later, when he was a political leader, he used the same tactic. "Even as a boy, I defeated my opponents without dishonoring them," he wrote many years later.

Mandela was a member of the Thembu tribe. The head of the tribe was the chief. The chief made the final decisions for the tribe. He also helped solve problems between members.

When Mandela was nine, his father died. Mandela went to live with the chief of the Thembu people. The chief began to prepare Mandela to serve as the royal adviser. He showed Mandela the duties of a tribe leader. He showed him how to make decisions.

*Mandela watched the chief. He saw how the chief would guide all members to agreement. The chief told him, "A leader is like a shepherd. He stays behind the flock, letting the most nimble go out ahead, whereupon the others follow, not realizing all along that they are being directed from behind."

One of the most important things Mandela learned was to listen to everyone. Only after everyone had spoken did the chief give his thoughts.

When Mandela was a little older, he went to a school run by English missionaries. He learned English there. He was also given a new name by a teacher. It was the name of a famous British hero—Nelson. When Mandela was 21 he went away to a university. The chief wanted Mandela to have a good education. Away from the village, he saw how Caucasians and black Africans were treated differently.

Mandela learned* some other lessons. The chief had picked a young woman for him to marry. But Mandela did not want to marry her. So he broke with custom and left the tribe. He left the life that had been set for him.

In 1941, when he was 23, Mandela moved to Johannesburg. Johannesburg was the most important city in South Africa. He finished his college studies by taking a course through the mail. And he went to work as a clerk in a law firm. He worked with a friend named Oliver Tambo.

In Johannesburg, Mandela faced the daily humiliation forced on all nonwhites. He was a proud man. He had been treated with great respect as a future leader of his tribe. In Johannesburg, he was reminded every day that he was not thought of as equal to Caucasians.

Mandela knew he must try to change the system. He later wrote, "There was no particular day on which I said, 'From henceforth I will devote myself to the liberation of my people;' instead, I simply found myself doing so, and could not do otherwise."

In 1944 he joined the African National Congress (ANC). The ANC was fighting for the equality of black Africans. By 1949 he was one of the party's leaders. The ANC tried to change things using nonviolent means.

At the same time, the South African government created the apartheid system. *Apartheid* was the rule of strictly segregating races. Before 1950, keeping the races separate was custom, but not law. In 1950 a law was passed that grouped all people by race. Business and living areas were segregated. Schools, hospitals, hotels, trains, and buses were segregated. Nonwhites were not allowed to enter areas designated for Caucasians.

In 1952 Mandela and Tambo opened a law firm. It was the first law firm in South Africa run by black Africans. That year the ANC led nonviolent protests in South Africa. They entered "whites only" areas. Mandela was arrested and found guilty. He was ordered not to go to public meetings.

In 1956 the government tried Mandela and 155 other people for *treason*, or plotting against the government. The trial lasted five years. In the end, they were found not guilty.

By 1960, riots in Sharpeville had killed 69 unarmed protesters. This changed the minds of many. Mandela and others decided nonviolence would not work in South Africa.

Soon the government banned the ANC, and a warrant was issued for Mandela's arrest. For a year he lived in secret as the police looked for him. He wore disguises. He went out only at night.

In 1962 Mandela was arrested and sent to prison. The next year, in a very famous trial, he was charged with plotting to violently overthrow the government.

In court, Mandela admitted some of the charges, even though it might have meant death. He said, "During my lifetime I have dedicated myself to the struggle of the African people. I have fought against white domination, and I have fought against black domination. I have cherished the ideal of a democratic and free society in which all persons live together in harmony and with equal opportunities. It is an ideal which I hope to live for and to achieve. But, if needs be, it is an ideal for which I am prepared to die."

Nelson Mandela visits a school in
Soweto, South Africa

In 1964 he was found guilty. He was sent to a prison on Robben Island for life. Mandela and others worked in the quarry there. They broke rocks most of the time. Through the years, Mandela never stopped planning for the day he would leave prison. He and others organized classes. They took courses through the mail. They created what was called the "Island University." And they sometimes sent messages to ANC leaders outside the prison. Mandela's friend Tambo ran the ANC from outside the country.

People from all over the world protested South African apartheid. Many countries would not do business with South Africa. Many people died in the fight against apartheid. And Mandela became a symbol of the fight for equality.

In the 1980s, the South African government made offers to Mandela. He decided to talk to them. In 1986 they began secret talks. Then Mandela was moved to a different prison where he had his own small house. In 1989 South Africa got a new president—F. W. de Klerk. The new president knew he must find a way to change the system. So he and Mandela talked together in person.

Mandela was the most famous political prisoner in the world. In February 1990 he was released. He had spent 27 years in prison. The next year Mandela became president of the ANC.

In 1993 Mandela and de Klerk won the Nobel Prize for Peace. In 1994 South Africa held its first election in which all races could vote. Mandela and the ANC won easily.

Mandela became president of South Africa. But his job was not easy. He had to help create a nation of many races in which all were equal. In 1999 Mandela retired from politics. He was 81 years old. But he has not stopped working for his country.

Chapter 4

Lech Walesa

One of the most important events of the 20th century was the end of the Soviet Union. The Soviet Union finally broke up in 1991. There were a lot of reasons this happened. A workers' strike in Poland was one of the first signs that change was possible. The strike was led by a popular electrician named Lech Walesa.

Walesa was born in 1943, during World War II. At that time the German army controlled Poland. His family lived in a small village where most people were farmers. When Walesa was born, his father was in a Nazi prison camp. When his father returned, he was in terrible health and soon died. Walesa was not even two years old. After the war, Poland was very poor. Much had been destroyed.

Around that time, the Soviet Union forced the countries of Eastern Europe, including Poland, to become Communist. Stores and factories were taken over by the government. Private property was taken away. The Communist Party ran everything, and the secret police were very powerful.

When Walesa was a boy, he would walk five kilometers to school. After school he would walk seven kilometers to church. He often got into trouble. He didn't want to be a farmer, but he didn't have the money to go to college. So when he was 16, he went to a training school.

There he was trained as an electrician and a mechanic. His teachers said he was a troublemaker. But he earned a permit. Then he got a job as a mechanic. He wanted something different, so he decided to move to the city.

Walesa bought a train ticket to Gydnia. On the way, he got off at the city of Gdansk. He was thirsty and wanted something to drink. There he saw a friend who worked in the huge Lenin Shipyard. He stayed in Gdansk and took a job as an electrician.

What seemed like an unimportant decision would later change the history of Poland. In 1968 many people were angry with the government. Students and others in Poland wanted more freedom. Workers were unhappy too. Many factories were dangerous. There was never enough food. Pay was very low. And there was no way for people to express their ideas. There were no real elections. Newspapers were run by the Communist Party. The workers' unions were run by the Communist Party too.

The government controlled the price of most things. In 1970 the government announced it would raise the prices of basic goods. At the Lenin Shipyard, about 1,000 workers—including Walesa—went on strike, even though it was illegal to do so. Workers in other cities went on strike too. Soon the protests turned into riots. Fights broke out between protesters and military forces. Many workers were killed.

During that strike, Walesa was elected to the strike committee. He tried to stop the fighting, but he could not. Later he said he learned many lessons from those riots.

In 1976, elections were held in Gdansk for the workers' union. Walesa gave a speech for the first time. He declared that workers' rights had to be protected. He said the shipyard management was unfair. He was soon fired from his job. Walesa then worked as a mechanic at different places. He became involved with groups that wanted independent trade unions. In 1979 he was again fired for his political activity.

In December 1979 some independent groups held a meeting on the anniversary of the riots of December 1970. Walesa gave a speech urging those who wanted change to come together and fight. That meeting marked the beginning of a new movement in Poland. Those who joined knew it was dangerous. Protesters were beaten by police and put in prison.

Reforming the system was a danger to the Polish government. It was also a test to Soviet control of Poland. Everyone knew the Soviet Union wanted to control the country. In Hungary in 1956 and Czechoslovakia in 1968 there had been protests and reform movements. Both times the Soviet army had invaded. There were already thousands of Soviet military troops in Poland.

In the summer of 1980, the government announced that prices would go up again. In August the workers at the Lenin Shipyard went on strike again. Walesa no longer worked there, but he climbed the wall of the shipyard to get in. He climbed on top of a bulldozer and gave a speech in front of thousands of striking workers.

Lech Walesa speaks to workers during
a strike in 1980

Walesa became the leader of the strike. He held talks with the government. The government agreed to some things. But many striking workers wanted the government to do more than just lower the price of meat and raise their wages. They wanted important political changes. And they wanted independent unions that would really act for the needs of the workers.

Walesa and the strike committee wrote a list of 21 demands for the government. The government soon agreed to many of the workers' demands. Walesa and the head of the Polish government signed an agreement on August 31, 1980.

Never before in any of the Soviet countries had workers reached a deal directly with the government. Around the world, people watched Walesa. They wondered what the changes in Poland might lead to. The union movement grew.

The Gdansk strike committee quickly changed into an independent union. It had members from all over the country. It was called Solidarity, and Walesa was its leader. By the next year, Solidarity had ten million members.

Walesa became as famous as many rock stars. The Solidarity flag and Walesa's mustache became symbols of hope where the government controlled so much of people's lives. Walesa went all over the world. He went to Rome to meet Pope John Paul II in January 1981. Pope John Paul II was from Poland. Walesa was very religious. The pope's support was important because many people in Poland were Roman Catholic. The Pope hoped the Communist system would change. He supported those changes every way he could.

At the same time, the Soviet Union was pressuring Polish leader General Jaruzelski to destroy Solidarity.

Finally the Polish government decided enough was enough. It wanted to stop the Solidarity movement. In December 1981 the government declared *martial law,* which meant the military would be in control of the government. It stopped all union activity. Public meetings became illegal. Thousands of Solidarity members, including Walesa, were put in jail.

*Walesa was held at a house in a small town. But he listened to the news on a radio that someone secretly brought to him. Martial law did not stop Solidarity. The union "went underground." It held secret meetings. Walesa was released in November 1982. He was carefully watched, but he continued to secretly meet with union members and other leaders.

Walesa was an international hero. In 1983 he won the Nobel Prize for Peace. But he could not leave Poland to accept the award. He feared he would not be allowed to return. So he asked his wife to accept the award for him.

Martial law was lifted in 1983, but life in Poland grew worse. By 1987 the government knew it was losing control. The economy was very bad. In 1988 new strikes spread across the country. The workers at the Lenin Shipyard went on strike again. Walesa* returned to lead the strike. But he was no longer the young union leader. He had turned into the older politician.

Then the government did something dramatic. It decided to work with Solidarity. The government knew it needed the union's help to keep the country from falling apart. And that meant talking with Walesa, Solidarity's leader.

And the situation was different in another way. There was a new leader in the Soviet Union: Mikhail Gorbachev. Gorbachev said he would not use the Soviet military against the strikers.

In 1989 the Polish government allowed Solidarity to become a political party. In June 1989 there were real elections. Solidarity won 99 of the 100 seats in the Polish parliament. The party that had been banned only eight years before now controlled the government. And in 1990, Walesa became president of Poland.

—Chapter 5—

Aung San Suu Kyi

Would you be willing to give up everything, including your family, to fight for freedom? A Burmese woman named Aung San Suu Kyi has spent most of her life away from her family, under house arrest. This is because she decided to struggle against a cruel government.

Suu Kyi was born in Rangoon, Burma, in 1945. Her father, General Aung San, did not do things the way others did. In Burma, parents usually do not give their own names to their children. But he gave his name to his two sons and to his daughter. *Aung San* means "victory." For his daughter, he added his mother's name, Suu, and his wife's name, Kyi. All together it means "bright collection of strange victories."

Aung San was a powerful military leader. He wanted to win freedom for his country. Burma, which is in southeastern Asia, was then part of the British Empire. Burma was a peaceful and fairly rich country. The general formed an army to fight for Burma's freedom from British rule. The army joined the Japanese during World War II to force the British out of Burma. The British left in 1942. Then, at the end of the war, Aung San joined the British to force out the Japanese!

Aung San's goal was always freedom for his country. But he never got to see his dream of a free Burma. He was murdered in 1947. Burma gained its independence in 1948, six months after he died.

Suu Kyi was only two years old when her father died. She spent her early years in the capital, Rangoon. When she was 15, her mother was named ambassador to India. Suu Kyi went to live there with her mother. Then she went to Oxford University in England.

While she was in India, the military took control of Burma. Many rights and freedoms were taken away from the Burmese people. Suu Kyi chose not to return. She moved to New York City to work at the United Nations. A man from England wanted to marry her. They wrote many letters to each other. In one of the letters, Suu Kyi agreed to marry him as long as he would support her if her people ever needed her. He agreed, and they were married.

The two settled in England, where they had two sons. Suu Kyi's husband became a professor at Oxford. She took care of their children. It seemed that her comfortable life in England would go on.

As her boys grew older, Suu Kyi searched for answers to her past. She wanted to know more about her father. For a year she lived in Japan to research his story. And she studied about him while living in India for a year with her husband and family.

In London in 1988, Suu Kyi got a phone call from Rangoon. Her mother had suffered a stroke. Suu Kyi left for Burma. She did not know then that she was leaving the life she knew behind—forever.

In Burma, students were protesting the government. In August 1988 thousands of people marched in the streets to show support for democracy. The police were told to shoot the protesters. After that, Suu Kyi knew she must take a stand.

Several weeks later, Suu Kyi stood on a stage and spoke to 100,000 people. She called the protests against the rulers a struggle for independence. The people cheered her speech. In a moment, she had become a leader of the pro-democracy group. She was 43 years old.

The government did not like the popularity of the pro-democracy group. In September 1988 the government declared martial law. Protesters filled the streets. Police fired into the crowds and chased those who ran away. Almost 3,000 people were killed in two months.

But that did not stop Suu Kyi and others. She helped start a new party—the National League for Democracy (NLD).

One day she went to a village during the election campaign. Suddenly, a group of soldiers stepped in front of her group and blocked their path. Suu Kyi told the group not to stop. She calmly asked the soldiers to please let them pass. Then she walked toward the soldiers. A major arrived and ordered the soldiers to let them pass. Later this story became famous. It gave hope to many people in Burma who were afraid of the military.

Everywhere Suu Kyi went, thousands came to hear her. She made it clear she was working for the kind of government her father would have wanted—a free, democratic Burma.

Finally, on July 20, 1989, the Burmese government placed her under house arrest. She could not leave her house. The government told her she would be freed if she left the country. But she refused to leave until all political prisoners were freed and the government was no longer run by the military. So she remained in her home. She could not campaign. The phone lines to her house were cut. After January 1990 her family was not allowed to visit her.

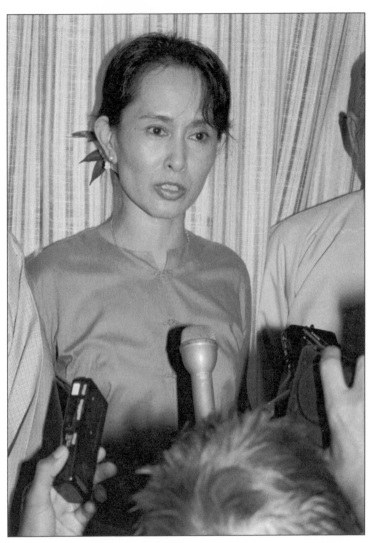

Aung San Suu Kyi holds her first news conference
after being released from house arrest in 1995

The military government had given the country a new name: Myanmar. Elections were held in May 1990. They were the first real elections in the country in 30 years. The NLD won 82 percent of the seats in the parliament. It was a great success. But the government would not accept the results. It refused to allow the new parliament to meet.

After July 1990, Suu Kyi was not allowed to write to her family. One day in 1991, Suu Kyi was listening to the news on the radio. She heard she had won the Nobel Prize for Peace. She knew she could not go to Europe to accept the award because the generals would not allow her to return to Burma. So her husband accepted the prize for her.

*For six years she could not leave her house. Her husband was only allowed to visit her twice. The government again told her she would be freed if she left the country. She refused. And so the generals and Suu Kyi remained in a standoff.

As the years passed, she followed a strict routine. She woke every day at 4:30 A.M. Because she was a Buddhist, she meditated for one hour. Then she exercised and dressed. She put a flower in her hair. She cleaned and sewed. She read. But the house around her slowly fell apart. The yard grew wild.

In July 1995 her house arrest was lifted. She spoke to supporters outside her house that day. She said she hoped the people and the government could work together. She compared their struggle with the struggle in South Africa. She felt that if they could do it, so could* her country.

Her husband and two sons were still in England. In January 1999 her husband was told he had cancer. He had not seen Suu Kyi for three years. The Burmese government would not give him a visa to visit her. If she went to England, she would not be allowed back. Her husband died without seeing his wife again.

Suu Kyi never stopped working for a democratic government. And the government never stopped bothering her. Crowds would find her wherever she went. In 2000 she was placed under house arrest again. It lasted until 2002.

Then, in May 2003, when she and a group went to a night rally, a mob attacked their car. The attackers were working for the government. They pushed sharpened bamboo sticks inside the car. Old women were beaten and stripped naked. Some were sent to prison. Nearly 200 people at the rally were killed or injured.

Suu Kyi was put in prison for four months. Then, once again, she was placed under house arrest.

In June 2005 Suu Kyi marked her 60th birthday. She still lives in her crumbling home. Her country is one of the poorest in the world. Its government has destroyed its economy and is still one of the harshest governments in the world. Thousands of political prisoners remain in jail. And Suu Kyi is still waiting for the day the generals are no longer afraid of her.

—Chapter 6—

The Dalai Lama

How does a poor nation fight for independence from one of the biggest countries in the world? If you are the Dalai Lama, you never stop working. But you might change your idea about what "independence" can mean.

The Dalai Lama, whose real name is Lhamo Thondup, was born in 1935 in a poor village in Tibet. Only about 20 families lived in a wide valley there. His parents grew grain and potatoes. They also raised animals that grazed in the high pastures. Thondup's family lived on whatever they raised. It was a hard life. His mother had 14 children, but only nine lived to be adults.

Tibet is on a very high plateau surrounded by mountains. Those high mountains have kept Tibet cut off from the rest of the world. Many who live there are *nomads*. This means they continually travel with their animals from one place to another.

*For hundreds of years, Tibet was controlled by Tibetan Buddhist monks. The head of the monks was the Dalai Lama. The Dalai Lama was the spiritual leader and often the political leader of Tibet.

Tibetan Buddhists believe that a person's soul is born again into a different body. So after an important religious leader dies, they look for the rebirth of that leader. The 13th Dalai Lama died in 1933. As is custom, a search began for the next Dalai Lama.

One day, when Thondup was two years old, two men came to his family's house. Thondup was interested in the two strangers. They began to ask him questions. When they showed him a group of objects, he picked out things that had belonged to the 13th Dalai Lama.

The two strangers were lamas searching for the 14th Dalai Lama. *Lamas* are Tibetan Buddhist monks. They said they were guided to Thondup's* home by a vision. There were also other signs that had led the lamas to that remote valley. The lamas decided that Thondup was the 14th Dalai Lama. He was taken to a Tibetan Buddhist monastery to prepare for his new role. It would be the most important role in Tibet.

When Thondup was five years old, he was named the Dalai Lama. He was then Tibet's religious leader. He lived in the Potala Palace. It is a 1,000-room palace in Lhasa, the capital of Tibet. His days were filled with studies. He was surrounded by the best and wisest teachers. Government advisers were always with him.

They were all preparing him to be the political leader of Tibet. But he was still a boy. He liked to play, but there were not many children around. So he played with the workers in the palace.

His life was very different from that of most Tibetans. When he left the palace, the people of Lhasa went to see him as he was carried around in his palanquin. A *palanquin* is like a covered bed that is carried on poles.

This very special life began to change when the Communist army took control of China in 1949. The army declared the "liberation" of Tibet. The Communists said Tibet was a part of China. The Dalai Lama was 14 years old at the time.

In October 1950 the Chinese army invaded eastern Tibet. The Dalai Lama asked the United Nations for help, but it refused. His advisers talked him into taking the political powers of his office. In November 1950, at age 15, the Dalai Lama became Tibet's head of state.

The Dalai Lama tried to work with the Chinese government. A group of Tibetans was called to China and forced to sign an agreement with the Chinese. It was supposed to guarantee Tibetan freedom.

China said it wanted to bring Tibet into the "modern world." It saw the Tibetan government as "backward." It wanted to destroy the power of the monks. Thousands of monks were tortured and killed. Hundreds of religious buildings were destroyed.

Protests in Lhasa against the Chinese grew. Many thought China was planning to kill the Dalai Lama. It was a dangerous situation. Finally, the Dalai Lama decided to leave Tibet.

In the spring of 1959, he dressed as a soldier. Then he passed through the crowd in front of the palace. He rode on horseback across the snow-covered passes of the Himalayas into India. There, he created a government outside Tibet. Meanwhile, the Chinese army violently put down the revolt in Lhasa.

Since 1960 the Dalai Lama's government has been based in Dharamsala, India. Many Tibetan refugees followed him there. The Dalai Lama also helped settle Tibetan refugees in many other places.

In his early life, the Dalai Lama was protected from the world. Later, he dove headfirst into it. Wearing his monk's red robes, he went all over the world to call attention to the situation in Tibet. He met with leaders from many countries.

In 1989 the Dalai Lama won the Nobel Prize for Peace. In his speech, he called himself "a simple monk from Tibet." He accepted the award in honor of Gandhi and on behalf of six million Tibetans. He said they faced "a strategy aimed at the destruction of their national and cultural identities."[1]

[1] © The Nobel Foundation 1989.

He said, "The suffering of our people during the past 40 years of occupation is well documented. Ours has been a long struggle. We know our cause is just. Because violence can only breed more violence and suffering, our struggle must remain nonviolent and free of hatred."[2]

He said that one-sixth of all Tibetans had died as a result of the Chinese attacks and occupation. He reminded others that Tibetans did not have basic human rights.

In many ways the Dalai Lama seems far from reaching his goals for Tibet. However, something interesting has happened. In 1959 almost no one in the West knew anything about Tibetan Buddhism. In fact, the 14th Dalai Lama was the first to travel to the West.

[2] © The Nobel Foundation 1989.

Since then, the Dalai Lama has become one of the most respected spiritual leaders of our time. And he has spread the teachings of and information about Tibetan Buddhism all over the world. Many Tibetan monks have moved to the United States, Canada, and Europe.

The Dalai Lama has also has written many books. A book he wrote with Howard Cutler called *The Art of Happiness* was on a bestseller list for over two years. There are now people all over the world who follow Tibetan Buddhism.

By 2001 the Dalai Lama had decided China would not let go of Tibet. China had a huge army. He knew Tibet could not fight it. Hundreds of thousands of Chinese troops were in Tibet. Tens of thousands of Chinese people had moved there. There were more Chinese in Lhasa than Tibetans.

The Dalai Lama decided Tibet did not have to be free from China. He wanted an agreement to keep Tibet as part of China, but only as long as they could keep their Tibetan culture. Some people were angry that he did not keep working for Tibetan independence. But he felt that trying to come to an agreement with China was better. They have still not come to an agreement, however.

In July 2005 the Dalai Lama had his 70th birthday. His people met with Chinese officials to try and work out a return visit for him. He had not seen his homeland since 1959. The Chinese did not allow him to return.